SYNAGOGUES
OF NEW YORK CITY

A Pictorial Survey in 123 Photographs

by
Oscar Israelowitz

DOVER PUBLICATIONS, INC.
NEW YORK

Published in Canada by General Publishing Company, Ltd., 30 Lesmill Road, Don Mills, Toronto, Ontario.
Published in the United Kingdom by Constable and Company, Ltd., 10 Orange Street, London WC2H 7EG.

Synagogues of New York City: A Pictorial Survey in 123 Photographs is a new work, first published by Dover Publications, Inc., in 1982.

Book Design by Paula Goldstein

International Standard Book Number: 0-486-24231-5
Library of Congress Catalog Card Number: 81-69678

Manufactured in the United States of America
Dover Publications, Inc.
180 Varick Street
New York, N.Y. 10014

Front Cover: B'nai Jeshurun, Manhattan.
Frontispiece: Sons of Israel Kalvarie, Manhattan.

CONTENTS

INTRODUCTION

The word synagogue refers both to the place where Jews assemble for worship, study and communal activities and to the congregation itself. The traditional synagogue structure is one that is a *mikdash me'at*, a miniature sanctuary, designed in the mode of the ancient Temple in Jerusalem. Although rabbinical authorities prescribed specific requirements for synagogue design, they have been open to interpretation over the course of time.

From a technical point of view, to have the status of a synagogue a structure need only be a place where at least ten Jews assemble regularly for prayer. There are some Halachic or rabbinical prescriptions of architectural details. The synagogue should be the tallest building in the city. This requirement is qualified in "difficult" situations such as when the Jews are the minority of the city's population.

The synagogue should have windows to allow worshippers to see the heavens and achieve a suitable frame of mind for prayer. The windows should face Jerusalem. According to one source, there should be 12, symbolic of the 12 tribes of Israel. The synagogue must have an ark, containing the Torah scrolls, placed against the wall facing Jerusalem (usually the eastern wall).

The Rambam, Maimonides, rules that the reading platform (*bimah* to the Ashkenazic; *alememar* to the Sephardic) must be located in the center of the synagogue so that the congregation should be able to hear the reading of the Torah. This was the customary practice until the Haskalah, or Enlightenment, of the early nineteenth century in Germany. The German Reform movement designed its synagogues and temples with the *bimah* placed along the eastern wall. Eventually it became the actual platform on which the ark also stood. The rabbis of Hungary and Galicia initially put a ban (*chayrem*) on this practice, but it spread and was adopted even among Orthodox congregations.

The traditional synagogue contains a separate section for women, in accordance with the practice in the ancient Temple in Jerusalem. There is also a *ner tamid*, a continuously burning lamp, symbolic of the eternal light which burned in the Temple.

Other than incorporating these features, there has never been an accepted form of architecture identified exclusively with the synagogue. It has always tended to reflect the community, the era and society in which it developed. Architects have designed synagogue buildings in the style of a Greek temple, a Byzantine mosque, a Gothic cathedral, a *shtetl* (village) synagogue of Eastern Europe and, more recently, in the form of a sculptural abstraction.

The first synagogue in New York was built in 1730 by the Congregation Shearith Israel. Modeled after the Great Sephardic (Spanish-Portuguese) Synagogue of Amsterdam, the modest masonry building measured about 30 x 30 feet, and was located on Mill (now South William) Street in the Wall Street district. The original building is no longer extant, but the reading platform and some of its other fittings are preserved in the present Shearith Israel building on Central Park West. The first synagogue's appearance is preserved in David Grim's "1742 Plan of New York" which illustrates it, along with a number of church buildings (*fig. 1*).

The Napoleonic Wars in the early nineteenth century witnessed the uprooting of entire Jewish communities in Germany and Poland. These Ashkenazic Jews migrated to New York and established such congregations as B'nai Jeshurun, Temple Emanu-El, Shaarey Hashomayim (Central Synagogue), Shaaray Tefila and Rodeph Sholom. At first, many of these congregations simply purchased existing Protestant church buildings and adapted them for use as their houses of worship. Since these buildings did not contain any statuary or idols, they were given rabbinical approval for use as synagogues.

As the congregations grew and moved to more fashionable areas, architects were commissioned to design new synagogue structures. The architectural styles reflected contemporary architectural trends and also showed the influence of the congregation's country of origin. The Jews migrating from Germany or Hungary in the mid-nineteenth century often built their new synagogues to resemble those left in the old country. Many of the synagogues of Berlin and Budapest were designed in the Moorish Revival style, which was influential in the design of New York's Temple Emanu-El, designed by Eidlitz and Fernbach in 1868 (*figs. 17 and 18*), and the Central Synagogue, designed by Henry Fernbach in 1872 (*fig. 9*). The former building is no longer extant.

The oldest surviving synagogue buildings in New York City belonged to Reform congregations and were patterned in the Gothic, a style associated with church architecture. Congregation Anshe Chesed's fourth location, on Norfolk Street on the Lower East Side of Manhattan, was designed by Alexander Saeltzer in 1849 and was the largest synagogue in New York at the time. This building still stands but has been abandoned (*fig. 10*). Brooklyn's oldest congregation, Temple Beth Elohim, was designed by William Ditmars in 1876, in High Victorian Gothic. Located in the Williamsburg section, it is now utilized by a Chasidic Hebrew school (*figs. 39 and 40*).

The mass immigration of Jews fleeing persecution in Eastern Europe between 1880 and 1920 set a new direction in synagogue architecture. Many of these immigrants lived in the *shtetls* of Poland and Russia where synagogue design was an evolutionary outgrowth of many centuries of traditional folk art. The architectural motifs of the traditional wooden synagogues of Eastern Europe were transplanted to New York after 1900. The surviving Shtetl Revival synagogue buildings of the Bronx (Montefiore Congregation, 1906, *fig. 81*) and Queens (First Independent Hebrew Congregation, 1905, *figs. 101 and 102*) and Temple of Israel (*fig. 92*) all share similar architectural characteristics. They are wood-frame structures, incorporating a twin-tower motif, and display onion domes above each tower.

The first American-born Jewish architect, Arnold Brunner, was a leading figure in New York synagogue design. Some of his architectural accomplishments include Congregation Anshe Chesed/Adas Jeshurun (1874), Educational Alliance (1889), Temple Beth El (1891), Shaare Tephila/West End Synagogue (1894), Shearith Israel (1897) and Temple Israel of Harlem (1907). Brunner's early works reflected a Romanesque style with Islamic and Byzantine elements. His design for Congregation Shearith Israel on Central Park West (*fig. 4*) was the turning point of his architectural philosophy. Brunner's new design returned to classical motifs, influenced greatly by the Greco-Roman style of the Galilean synagogues, particularly that of Bar'am, near K'far Birim, excavated by the Palestine Exploration Fund in 1886 (*fig. 3*).

The period following World War I witnessed a near-total halt in immigration and a dispersal of the existing Jewish population to almost every area of New York City. A postwar housing boom was accompanied by a synagogue-construction boom. The architectural styles utilized in these synagogues ranged from Neoclassical to eclectic, an amalgam of every conceivable architectural idiom.

This period marked the birth of the Jewish Center movement. As a deterrent to assimilation and intermarriage with gentiles by second-generation American Jews, Rabbi Mordecai Kaplan introduced the concept of the Jewish Center, which would provide the young people of the community with a religious context for their own social gatherings. These modern synagogues sponsored youth groups, social clubs, dances, athletic events and other attractive activities that brought young Jewish adults together. The Jewish Center concept was influential in the development of the Conservative Movement in the United States. The first Jewish Center, designed by Louis Allen Abramson in 1919, is located on West 86th Street, on the Upper West Side of Manhattan (*fig. 32*).

It was not until after World War II that the architectural style of the synagogue was no longer influenced by the ecclesiastical motifs of the past. New materials and technology, coupled with stylistic freedom, have created a new genre of synagogue design. Architects have been guided by the watchword of the modern school of architecture, "form follows function." The contemporary synagogue of New York reflects multiple functions contained under one roof. Spatial requirements include such items as the sanctuary, Hebrew school, social hall, gymnasium, catering facilities and parking areas.

The noted synagogue architect Percival Goodman has designed over 50 synagogues throughout the United States. In his Temple Israel of Staten Island, Goodman embodied the teachings of the Brutalist School, incorporating exposed structural details of concrete, brick and wood, with an open, flexible plan, creating a sculptural abstraction (*fig. 116*). Discarding the elaborate ornaments of earlier architectural periods and styles, the synagogue architect has developed a more direct and honest approach to creating functional design.

The centrality of the Torah in Jewish life has been reflected in several contemporary New York synagogue designs. The Lincoln Square Synagogue in Manhattan, designed in 1970 by Hausman & Rosenberg (*figs. 35 and 36*), the Salanter Akiba Riverdale (SAR) Academy chapel in the Bronx, designed by Caudill, Rowlett, Scott, Associates in 1974 (*fig. 89*) and Congregation Knesseth Israel (White Shul) in Far Rockaway, Queens, designed by Kelly and Gruzen (*fig. 100*), share similar architectural features. They all reflect the belief that the Torah is the central core of Jewish life and have therefore been designed as theaters in the round, with the *bimah* in the center. The contemporary synagogue of New York reflects the synthesis of the traditional rabbinical guidelines blended with the expression of stylistic freedom.

Synagogues Listed in the Text

This listing includes
either the current or last location
of a congregation.

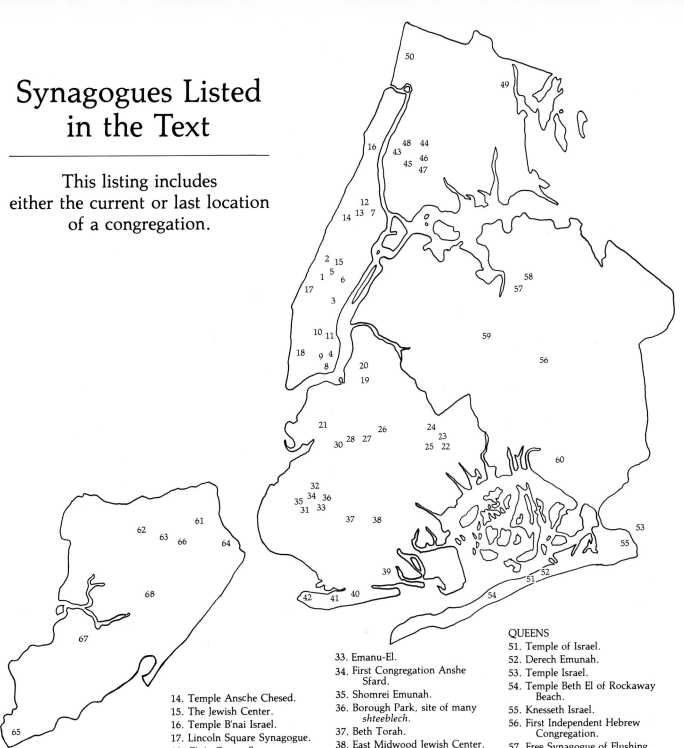

MANHATTAN
1. Shearith Israel.
2. Central Synagogue.
3. Shaarey Hashomayim.
4. Anshe Chesed.
5. Rodeph Sholom.
6. Temple Emanu-El.
7. Shaare Zedek of Harlem.
8. Sons of Israel Kalvarie.
9. Kahal Adath Jeshurun.
10. B'nai Rappaport.
11. Bais Hamedrash Hagadol Anshe Ungarin.
12. Temple Israel of Harlem.
13. Ohab Zedek.
14. Temple Ansche Chesed.
15. The Jewish Center.
16. Temple B'nai Israel.
17. Lincoln Square Synagogue.
18. Civic Center Synagogue.

BROOKLYN
19. Temple Beth Elohim.
20. Ohav Sholom.
21. Baith Israel Anshei Emes.
22. Agudas Achim B'nai Jacob.
23. Chevre Chayei Adam.
24. Temple Sinai.
25. Ohab Sholom.
26. Shaare Zedek.
27. Brooklyn Jewish Center.
28. Union Temple.
29. Park Slope Jewish Center.
30. Beth Elohim.
31. Temple Beth El.
32. Torath Moshe.
33. Emanu-El.
34. First Congregation Anshe Sfard.
35. Shomrei Emunah.
36. Borough Park, site of many *shteeblech.*
37. Beth Torah.
38. East Midwood Jewish Center.
39. B'nai Israel.
40. Sea Breeze Jewish Center.
41. Shaare Zedek.
42. Kneses Israel.

THE BRONX
43. Temple Adath Israel.
44. Beth Hamedrash Hagadol Adath Israel of the Bronx.
45. Montefiore Congregation.
46. Sons of Israel.
47. Sinai Congregation.
48. Mount Eden Center.
49. Co-op City, site of six synagogues.
50. Salanter Akiba Riverdale Academy.

QUEENS
51. Temple of Israel.
52. Derech Emunah.
53. Temple Israel.
54. Temple Beth El of Rockaway Beach.
55. Knesseth Israel.
56. First Independent Hebrew Congregation.
57. Free Synagogue of Flushing.
58. Temple Gates of Prayer.
59. Forest Hills Jewish Center.
60. International Synagogue.

STATEN ISLAND
61. New Brighton Jewish Congregation.
62. Temple Emanu-El.
63. Agudath Achim Anshe Chesed.
64. Tifereth Israel.
65. Ahavath Israel.
66. Temple Israel Reform Congregation.
67. Arden Heights Boulevard Jewish Center.
68. Young Israel of Staten Island.

Manhattan

The founders of the Jewish community of New York were members of the Dutch West India Company. Expelled from a colony in Recife, Brazil because of their religious beliefs, the group of 23 Jews found their way to the Dutch colony of New Amsterdam (later New York) in 1654. The antisemitic governor, Peter Stuyvesant, admitted the refugees only after pressure was applied by the Dutch West India Company in Amsterdam, whose principal shareholders were Jewish. Although these refugees did establish the first synagogue in North America in 1654, it was not until 1730 that the first building constructed specifically as a synagogue was dedicated.

Congregation Shearith Israel was the first and only synagogue in Manhattan from 1654 to 1825. During that period it served the Jewish community, which included both Sephardic Jews (those of Spanish and Portuguese descent) and Ashkenazic (those of German and Polish descent). In the 1820s, the substantial influx of German and Polish Jews fleeing the upheavals of the Napoleonic Wars led to dissidence in the congregation, and New York's first wholly Ashkenazic congregation, B'nai Jeshurun, was established in 1825.

This break from the "mother congregation" set the trend for the creation of other new synagogues. Dutch, Polish and German seceders from B'nai Jeshurun organized Anshe Chesed in 1828. Further splits led to the formation of Shaare Zedek by Poles and Shaarey Hashomayim by Germans in 1839. Other German Jews who quit Anshe Chesed and Shaarey Hashomayim organized Rodeph Sholom in 1842. Wealthier Germans moving toward substantial ritual reform founded Temple Emanu-El in 1845.

The Berlin Haskalah (Enlightenment) of the early nineteenth century was the birth of the Reform movement. In Germany, where the Reform movement became institutionalized in the 1840s, the theological rationalization went as far as to abolish not only the dietary laws but even circumcision and belief in the Messiah. Although its more radical preachings were not adopted at its outset, the Haskalah did have its impact on the American Jewish community. German Reform Jews who emigrated to New York at this time established these principles in their congregations. Their ideology struck roots with such rapidity that by 1880, before the waves of immigration of Orthodox Jews from Eastern Europe, the majority of the 200 synagogues in the entire United States embraced Reform Judaism. The synagogues designed in New York adopted the architectural styles, such as Gothic and Moorish Revival, employed in the Reform synagogues of Germany.

The Jewish settlement of Manhattan closely paralleled the growth of the city. During the 1830s the major Jewish concentrations were in Lower Manhattan, near the Lower East Side. By 1850, the Jewish population of New York was 50,000 and had moved as far north as 34th Street. As new sections became more fashionable, the prosperous German Jews moved uptown. These "uptown Jews" established sister communities in such areas as the Upper East Side, Harlem and the Upper West Side. At the turn of the century it was common to find a synagogue such as Congregation Shaare Zedek in the Lower East Side with an uptown branch in Harlem. Eventually, the downtown branch would also move uptown, abandoning the old neighborhood. However, the synagogues left behind remained vacant only briefly. The vacuum created was quickly filled by the continuous influx of Jewish immigrants fleeing pogroms, revolutions, wars, economic discrimination and social degradation in Eastern Europe.

Between 1880 and 1924 more than two million Jews emigrated to New York. They came with their entire families and, in many instances, with their entire communities. They established over 600 synagogues, some of which occupied the synagogue buildings left behind by the previous groups of Jews who moved uptown, but most of which were of the storefront or back-room (*shteebl*) variety, organized according to the old-country town of origin. When these new immigrants moved to the outlying boroughs of Queens and

1

Brooklyn at the turn of the century, they constructed some of their new synagogue buildings in the Shtetl Revival style of architecture.

With the completion of the new subway system and the subsequent housing boom, there was a mass dispersal from Manhattan to the Bronx, Queens and Brooklyn. The last major Jewish population shift within the city was in the 1920s. In the heyday of Harlem there were over 100,000 Jews living there. The deteriorating living conditions and the mass influx of black and Hispanic people into the area shifted the Jewish community to the Upper West Side and Washington Heights. Today there are an estimated 170,000 Jews in Manhattan, which has a total population of 1.5 million (1970).

CONGREGATION SHEARITH ISRAEL (SPANISH AND PORTUGUESE SYNAGOGUE), 99 Central Park West; 1897; Brunner & Tryon, architects. Figs. 1-6; Inside Back Cover, Top.

The oldest Jewish congregation in North America, Shearith Israel was organized in the Dutch settlement of New Amsterdam in 1654. The first structure built expressly as a synagogue for the congregation was erected in 1730 on Mill Street (now South William Street, near the New York Stock Exchange; *fig. 2*). The earliest known depiction of the building was in David Grim's 1742 plan of New York *(fig. 1)*. Although the building no longer stands, the original Colonial furnishing and religious ornaments, including *bimah* and floorboards, have been incorporated in the Little Synagogue, which adjoins the main building of the present Shearith Israel *(inside back cover, top)*. Virtually a replica of the Mill Street synagogue, it is used for the congregation's daily services. Parts of the later synagogue buildings of the congregation at 56 Crosby Street and 5 West 19th Street have also been preserved in the present building. In keeping with the tradition of not representing human images, the windows of the synagogue were designed by Louis Comfort Tiffany in simple, yet elegant patterns *(fig. 6)*. The main structure was designed in the Neoclassical style *(figs. 4 and 5)*, Arnold Brunner having been influenced by the discovery of the Galilean synagogue at Bar'am *(fig. 3)*.

CONGREGATION B'NAI JESHURUN, 257 West 88th Street, 1918; Hert & Schneider, architects. Figs. 7 and 8; Front Cover.

This, the oldest Ashkenazic synagogue in New York City, was organized in 1825 in a rebellious breakaway from the only existing congregation in the city, Shearith Israel. B'nai Jeshurun's first home was the former First Coloured Presbyterian Church at 112 Elm Street *(fig. 8)*. The building no longer stands. The present structure *(fig. 7)* is the fifth to house the congregation.

CONGREGATION AHAVAT CHESED SHAAREY HASHO-MAYIM/CENTRAL SYNAGOGUE, 652 Lexington Avenue, 1872; Henry Fernbach, architect. Fig.9; Inside Front Cover.

Having been organized by a Bohemian Reform congregation in 1839, Central Synagogue is an official New York City, State and National Historic Landmark, the oldest Jewish house of worship in continuous service in the state, and is the finest extant example of the Moorish Revival style in the city.

CONGREGATION ANSHE CHESED, 172 Norfolk Street, 1849; Alexander Saeltzer, architect. Fig. 10.

The fourth house of worship of the congregation that had been formed in 1828 by Dutch, Poles and Germans who had seceded from Congregation B'nai Jeshurun, this was the largest synagogue in the city when it was opened in 1849. After the congregation merged with Temple Beth El (which subsequently merged with Temple Emanu-El) the building, in the Gothic Revival style, was used by Congregation Ohab Zedek (1874) and finally by Congregation Anshe Slonim (1921-75). Now abandoned, it is threatened with demolition.

CONGREGATION RODEPH SHOLOM, 7 West 83rd Street, 1930; Charles B. Meyers, architect. Figs. 11-16.

The congregation was organized on the Lower East Side in 1842. Its building at 8 Clinton Street, erected in 1853 *(figs. 11 and 12)*, is the second-oldest surviving synagogue structure in the city. Rodeph Sholom subsequently moved to Lexington Avenue at East 63rd Street and to 130 West 56th Street. Congregation Chasam Sofer is now housed in the Clinton Street synagogue.

TEMPLE EMANU-EL, Fifth Avenue and East 65th Street, 1929; Kohn, Butler, Stein, architects, with Murray & Philip, consultants. Figs. 17-22.

Temple Emanu-El was organized in 1845, when services were conducted in a rented apartment on the Lower East Side. In 1848 the congregation moved to a little Neo-Romanesque structure at 56 Chrystie Street that had housed a Methodist congregation. Later synagogue buildings occupied by Emanu-El were a Gothic Revival former Baptist church (with steeple) on East 12th Street and the Moorish-style building (designed by Eidlitz and Fernbach) erected by the congregation in 1868 on Fifth Avenue and East 43rd Street *(figs. 17 and 18)*. In 1927 Temple Beth El consolidated with Emanu-El. Built in 1891 after designs by Arnold Brunner, Beth El *(fig. 19)* had graced Fifth Avenue's mansion row until it was demolished to make way for an apartment building. Congregation Anshe Chesed had previously merged with Beth El. The present structure of Temple Emanu-El *(figs. 20-22)* has a Gothic feeling (even though the architects drew upon the repertories of Romanesque, Byzantine and Art Deco as well as the Gothic), perhaps because of its loftiness. The interior carries out the same mode. The ceiling *(fig. 22)* is highly decorative. Steel trusses rest upon self-supporting bearing walls. The interior space of the main sanctuary is 77 feet wide, 150 feet long and 103 feet high. Adjoining the main sanctuary is the Beth El Chapel *(fig. 20)*. The stained-glass windows were designed by Louis Comfort Tiffany for the original building.

CONGREGATION SHAARE ZEDEK OF HARLEM, 23-25 West 118th Street, 1900; Michael Bernstein, architect. Fig. 23.

Originating in the Lower East Side in 1837, the congregation moved to this structure in Harlem before settling in its present location at 210 West 93rd Street in 1922.

CONGREGATION SONS OF ISRAEL KALVARIE, 15 Pike Street, 1903. Fig. 24.

In 1910 part of this congregation moved from the Lower East Side to form a sister congregation at 107 West 116th Street in Harlem.

CONGREGATION KAHAL ADATH JESHURUN (EL-DRIDGE STREET SYNAGOGUE), 12 Eldridge Street, 1886; Herter Bros., architects. Fig. 25.

The architect combined a Gothic rose window, Moorish horseshoe arches and a Romanesque facade. This was the first major New York synagogue built by Eastern European Jews, most previous structures having been erected by German-Jewish immigrants. It is now an official New York City landmark.

CONGREGATION B'NAI RAPPAPORT, East 7th Street near Avenue C, ca. 1900; Fig. 26.

This is the remains of a tenement synagogue. The animals carved in bas-relief in the cornice are mentioned in Biblical verses.

CONGREGATION BAIS HAMEDRASH HAGADOL AN-SHE UNGARIN, East 7th Street near Avenue D, 1895. Fig. 27.

The abandoned building is one of the few reminders of the Jewish community of the Lower East Side, north of Houston Street.

TEMPLE ISRAEL OF HARLEM, Lenox Avenue and West 120th Street, 1907; Arnold Brunner, architect. Figs. 28 and 29.

Once one of the most prestigious synagogues in the city, this Neo-Roman structure dates from the period when a number of German-Jewish families took up residence in the area's town houses which had been occupied by families of Dutch, English and Irish descent. Although Orthodox when it had been organized as the Hand-in-Hand Congregation in 1873, the congregation adopted the Reform ritual in 1888, changing its name to Temple Israel. It moved from the Lenox Avenue Building to 210 West 91st Street (now occupied by the Young Israel of the West Side) and finally to its present home at 112 East 75th Street in 1966.

CONGREGATION OHAB ZEDEK, 18 West 116th Street, 1908; Fig. 30.

The first home of the First Hungarian Congregation Ohab Zedek, which had been founded in 1873, was at 172 Norfolk Street in the synagogue that had formerly belonged to Congregation Anshe Chesed. In 1908, after many of its members had migrated uptown to then-fashionable Harlem, Ohab Zedek purchased its branch at 18 West 116th Street. The world-famous cantor Yossele Rosenblatt was engaged in 1912; he officiated in the Harlem synagogue for many years. In the 1920s many Jews left Harlem and in 1926 the congregation moved to its present location at 118 West 95th Street.

TEMPLE ANSCHE CHESED, 1881 Seventh Avenue, 1908; Edward I. Shire, architect. Fig. 31.

Organized in 1876, the temple moved to the Upper West Side in 1921. Its present home is on West End Avenue and West 100th Street.

THE JEWISH CENTER, 131 West 86th Street, 1919; Louis Allen Abramson, architect. Fig. 32.

Rabbi Mordecai Kaplan created the center as a deterrent to assimilation and intermarriage with gentiles by second-generation American Jews by providing the community with a Jewish context for social gatherings. It sponsored youth groups, social clubs and athletic events for young adults. Although the Jewish Center was influential in the development of the Conservative Movement in the United States, it follows the Orthodox ritual.

TEMPLE B'NAI ISRAEL (SHEARITH JUDAH), 610 West 149th Street, 1920. Figs. 33 and 34.

Jews moving out of Harlem in the 1920s settled not only on the Upper West Side, but in Washington Heights as well. The building is now a church.

LINCOLN SQUARE SYNAGOGUE, 200 Amsterdam Avenue, 1970; Hausman & Rosenberg, architects. Figs. 35 and 36.

Reaffirming the Torah as the central core of Jewish life, the architects designed the structure as a theater in the round. The synagogue is active in providing specifically designed educational and social programs for young people who have little or no religious background.

CIVIC CENTER SYNAGOGUE (CONGREGATION SHAARE ZEDEK), 49 White Street, 1967; William N. Berger Associates, architects. Figs. 37 and 38.

Located in the historic Cast-Iron District, the Civic Center Synagogue seems to float between two adjoining buildings. The area was the home of New York's first Sephardic synagogue, Congregation Shearith Israel, and of the first Ashkenazic synagogue, Congregation B'nai Jeshurun. Sweatshops and warehouses later filled the neighborhood. Today there are many residential lofts in this section south of Canal Street, known as Tribeca.

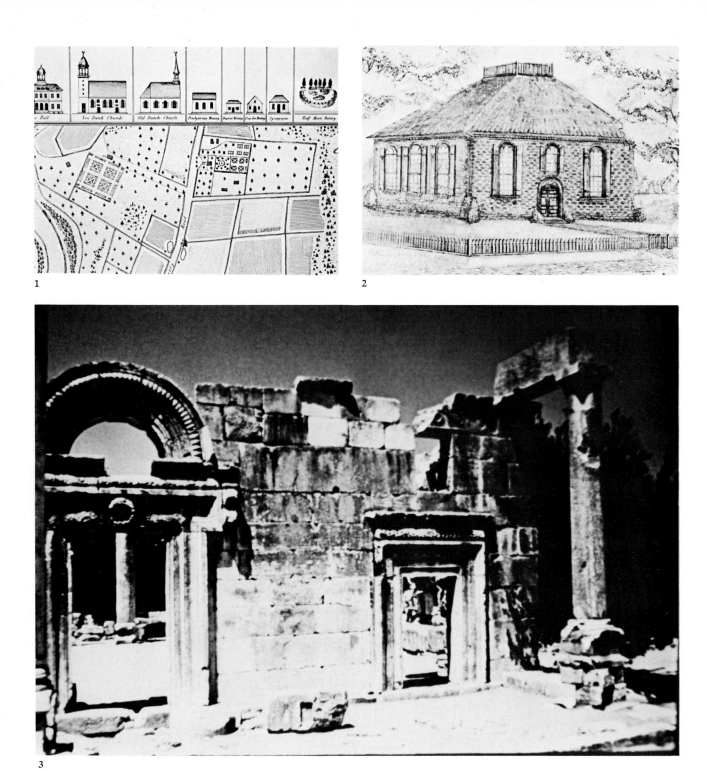

Shearith Israel. 1. First structure, on Mill Street, in David Grim's depiction of 1742. 2. The Mill Street synagogue. 3. Synagogue at Bar'am, inspiration for the present structure. 4. Facade of the present structure, 99 Central Park West. 5. Interior.

4

4

5

6

7

8

Shearith Israel. 6. Tiffany windows in the Little Synagogue.
B'nai Jeshurun, 257 West 88th Street. 7. Detail of ceiling. 8. Original Elm Street building.
Ahavat Chesed Shaarey Hashomayim (Central Synagogue), 652 Lexington Avenue. 9. Principal facade.

10

12

Anshe Chesed, 172 Norfolk Street. 10. Facade.
Rodeph Sholom. 11. Detail of door at original structure,
8 Clinton Street, showing Star of David. 12. The first
structure, in a woodcut of the time. 13. Facade of the
present structure, 7 West 83rd Street. 14. Detail of the
coffered ceiling. 15. Detail of the facade.

11

13

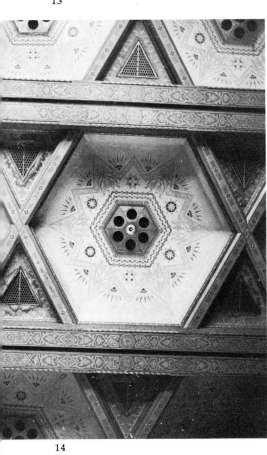

14

15

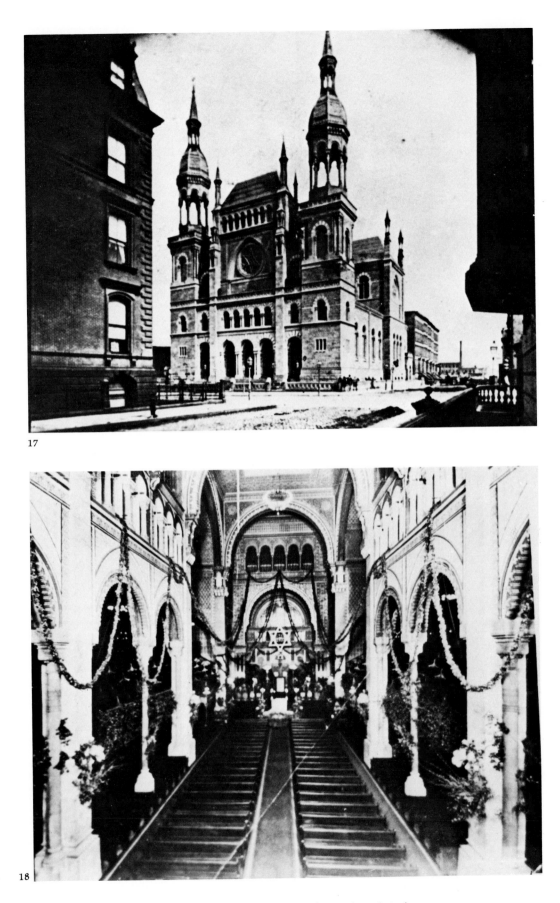

Rodeph Sholom. 16. View of the present structure's spacious interior.
Emanu-El. 17. The Moorish-style structure erected by the congregation in 1868, Fifth Avenue and East 43rd Street (demolished). 18. Interior of the 1868 building.

19

20

21

22

Emanu-El. 19. The 1891 building of Temple Beth El, a congregation which merged with Emanu-El in the 1940s, Fifth Avenue at 76th Street. **20.** The interior of the Beth-El Chapel in the present structure, Fifth Avenue and East 65th Street. **21.** The main facade. **22.** Detail of the ceiling of the main sanctuary.
Shaare Zedek of Harlem, 23–25 West 118th Street. **23.** Facade of the turn-of-the-century structure.

Sons of Israel Kalvarie, 15 Pike Street. 24. Principal facade.
Kahal Adath Jeshurun, 12 Eldridge Street. 25. Detail of the facade.

26

27

B'nai Rappaport, East 7th Street near Avenue C. 26. The remains of the facade.
Bais Hamedrash Hagadol Anshe Ungarin, East 7th Street near Avenue D. 27. Facade of the abandoned building.
Israel of Harlem, Lenox Avenue and West 120th Street. 28. View of the 1907 structure. 29. Interior of the Neoclassical sanctuary.

28

29

17

30

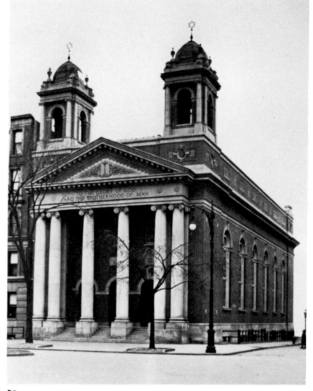

31

Ohab Zedek, 18 West 116th Street. 30. Exterior of the congregation's second location.

Ansche Chesed, 1881 Seventh Avenue. 31. View of the temple's facade.

The Jewish Center, 131 West 86th Street. 32. Exterior of the center, which provides a context for Jewish social activities.

B'nai Israel, 610 West 149th Street. 33. The dome and cornice, constructed in 1920. 34. Detail of the facade showing Jewish motifs.

32

33

34

37

38

Lincoln Square Synagogue, 200 Amsterdam Avenue. 35. Exterior of the building constructed in 1970. 36. The sanctuary's modernistic interior.
Civic Center Synagogue, 49 White Street. 37. Interior. 38. View of the structure's facade, which "floats" between adjoining nineteenth-century structures.

Brooklyn

There are an estimated 514,000 Jews living in Brooklyn, the borough in which half of all the synagogues in New York City are located. Jewish settlement in Brooklyn started in the 1830s. The two dominant communities were established in the Borough Hall section and in Williamsburg. During that period, Orthodox Jews would row across the East River to attend Sabbath services in Manhattan on Friday afternoon and return to Brooklyn on Sunday. In 1850, the first Jewish congregation was organized in Williamsburg by a group of German Jews. Kahal Kodesh Beth Elohim, later called Temple Beth Elohim, followed the Orthodox tradition at its outset. However, with the completion of its elegant temple on Keap Street in 1876, it adopted the Reform ritual. As a result of the shift of the Jewish population throughout Brooklyn, two of the oldest congregations, Temple Beth Elohim and Temple Israel (established in 1869), were merged in 1921, forming the Union Temple, which is now located in the Park Slope section of Brooklyn.

In Borough Hall, Congregation Baith Israel, organized in 1854, built Long Island's first synagogue in 1862 on the southeast corner of State Street and Boerum Place. The first rabbi of the congregation was Aaron Wise, father of Dr. Stephen S. Wise. When industry encroached on the neighborhood, the congregation was forced to look for a more fitting location to hold its services. In 1905, the congregation purchased the Trinity German Lutheran Church on Kane Street, in Cobble Hill, merged with the Talmud Torah Anshei Emes, and formed Congregation Baith Israel Anshei Emes. The original building is no longer extant.

The years between 1880 and 1920, marked by devastating wars and Czarist pogroms, formed one of the harshest periods for Jews living in Eastern Europe. Hundreds of thousands of immigrants poured into this country. The first stop for these immigrants was the Lower East Side of Manhattan, where their dreams of coming to an America where the streets were paved with gold were quickly shattered. The overcrowded and unsanitary living conditions, in which ten people would share one room in a cold-water flat, created the incentive for many to move out as soon as they could earn enough money. Many did and started life anew in the Brooklyn suburb communities of Crown Heights, Borough Park and Flatbush.

The earliest large-scale Jewish settlement started in 1885 when Jacob Cohen, a textile manufacturer, moved to a small town in East Brooklyn, Brown's Village, because of his wife's poor health. He moved his entire factory, brought his workers with him and started a self-contained Jewish community. This marked the beginning of Brownsville, a section once called the "Jerusalem of America." It was a city within a city, with over 200 synagogues and seven Hebrew schools. Today there is but one surviving synagogue in the entire section.

The construction of the elevated and subway lines extending into the heartland of Brooklyn between 1889 and 1920 enabled the new suburbanites to live as far away from the city factories and sweatshops as possible yet still afforded them easy access into the city to earn their daily bread.

The hot summer months brought the Jewish inhabitants of Brooklyn to the beaches. New Jewish congregations at Coney Island, Manhattan and Brighton Beach were established to meet the needs of the summer-resort Jewish communities. The summer synagogues would close after the vacation period. At the turn of the century, however, people realized the year-round beauty of these areas and the temporary communities, as well as their synagogues, soon became permanent establishments.

TEMPLE BETH ELOHIM, 274 Keap Street, 1876; William B. Ditmars, architect. Figs. 39 and 40.

Organized in 1850 as Kahal Kodesh Beth Elohim, this was the first congregation in Brooklyn and followed the Orthodox tradition. With the construction of this High Victorian synagogue building, the congregation changed its name to Temple Beth Elohim, adopting the Reform ritual. The congregation merged with Temple Israel in 1921 to form Union Temple. The original building, the oldest surviving synagogue structure in Brooklyn, is now used by a Chasidic yeshiva, Talmud Torah Pride of Israel.

CONGREGATION OHAV SHOLOM, 135 Thatford Avenue, 1906. Fig. 41.

Brownsville's synagogue history began in 1889 when Congregation Ohav Sholom was organized in the Watkins Avenue tailor shop of Elias Kaplan. The 1906 Shtetl Revival structure, near Belmont Street, was the largest in Brownsville. Notable spiritual leaders of the congregation included Rabbi Simon Finkelstein, Cantor David Roitman (with the Leove Choir), and Cantor Leibele Glantz. The synagogue is no longer extant.

CONGREGATION BAITH ISRAEL ANSHEI EMES, 236 Kane Street, 1856. Figs. 42–45.

Organized in 1856, Congregation Baith Israel built the first synagogue on Long Island in 1862 at the southeast corner of State Street and Boerum Place (*fig. 42*). That building is no longer extant; on its site stands the Brooklyn House of Detention. The congregation purchased the Trinity German Lutheran Church (originally the Middle Dutch Reformed Church) on Kane Street in 1905, merged with the Talmud Torah Anshei Emes to form Congregation Baith Israel Anshei Emes. The Neoclassical ark from its first synagogue has been preserved in the congregation's new home.

CONGREGATION AGUDAS ACHIM B'NAI JACOB, 503 Glenmore Avenue, 1921. Fig. 46.

Brownsville was once known as the "Jerusalem of America." Of the more than 200 synagogues in the Brownsville–East New York area in the 1940s, there remain only about a dozen structures today, most of them having been purchased by local churches.

CONGREGATION CHEVRE CHAYEI ADAM, 336 Ashford Street, ca. 1900. Fig. 47.

This building has gone through a cycle reflecting the changes of the neighborhood. Designed as a church, it was purchased by the congregation in 1914. In the 1960s it was sold to a Baptist church.

TEMPLE SINAI, 24 Arlington Avenue, 1920. Fig. 48.

Organized in the late 1880s as Congregation Bikur Cholim, Temple Sinai is all that remains of a once-thriving Jewish community. It is the last surviving active synagogue in Brownsville.

CONGREGATION OHAB SHOLOM, 19 Varet Street, 1905. Fig. 49.

The arrival of hundreds of thousands of East European Jews after 1900, combined with demolition of entire blocks of Lower East Side tenements in Manhattan to make way for the Williamsburg Bridge in 1903, caused a great surge of Jewish migration to Williamsburg, directly across the East River. The grand opening celebration of Congregation Ohab Sholom, complete with banners and American flags, marked the arrival of these new immigrants. The building has been demolished and today the area is predominantly Hispanic.

CONGREGATION SHAARE ZEDEK, Kingston Avenue and Park Place, 1924; Eisendrath & Horowitz, architects. Fig. 50.

Crown Heights was once the home of many wealthy Jews, many of whose mansions remain. The synagogue has been sold to a local church.

BROOKLYN JEWISH CENTER, 667 Eastern Parkway, 1920; Louis Allen Abramson, architect. Figs. 51–53.

The second Jewish center in the United States was a direct outgrowth of Manhattan's Jewish Center, which had been built in 1919. Containing facilities for religious, cultural, social and athletic activities, it was built at the then-staggering cost of $1 million. Notable spiritual leaders included Rabbi Dr. Israel H. Levinthal and Cantor Richard Tucker, who went on to a brilliant career as an opera singer (*fig. 53*).

UNION TEMPLE, 17 Eastern Parkway, 1926. Fig. 54.

As a result of the shifting population in Brooklyn, two of the old congregations, Temple Beth Elohim (1850) and Temple Israel (1869) merged in 1921 to form Union Temple. An 11-story structure, it contains a synagogue-auditorium with frescoed ceiling, as well as social rooms and a complete gymnasium. Arnold Brunner designed an adjoining synagogue building, but the Crash of 1929 cancelled all future construction plans, including the elaborate structure at the left of the illustration.

PARK SLOPE JEWISH CENTER (Congregation B'nai Jacob Tifereth Israel), Eighth Avenue and 14th Street, 1925. Fig. 55.

CONGREGATION BETH ELOHIM, Eighth Avenue and Garfield Place, 1909. Figs. 56 and 57.

Congregation Beth Elohim (not to be confused with Temple Beth Elohim in Williamsburg), Brooklyn's first Reform synagogue, was founded in 1861 by 48 dissident members of Congregation Baith Israel. It made several moves through Brooklyn Heights before settling in Park Slope. The congregation's pulpit is Brooklyn's oldest in continuous use.

TEMPLE BETH EL, 4802 Fifteenth Avenue, 1920; Shampan & Shampan, architects. Figs. 58–61; Back Cover.

Organized for the suburban community of Borough Park in 1902, Temple Beth Israel built its first synagogue in the Shtetl Revival style at 4022 Twelfth Avenue in 1906 (*fig. 58 and back cover*). The building is now occupied by Congregation Anshe Lubawitz. With the construction of the elevated subway lines in 1916 and the subsequent housing boom, the congregation moved to its present larger and more elegant quarters. The new structure, built in the Moorish Revival style, was directly influenced by Manhattan's Congregation B'nai Jeshurun. The auditorium (*figs. 60 and 61*) was engineered to have perfect acoustics. Notable spiritual leaders included Rabbi Dr. Israel Schorr and Cantors Hershman, Moshe Koussevitski and Moshe Stern.

CONGREGATION TORATH MOSHE, Tenth Avenue and 43rd Street, 1928; Fig. 62.

Although this congregation still functions, the immediate surrounding area is Hispanic. The stained-glass windows have been shattered and the meticulously detailed terra-cotta facade has been vandalized with spray paint.

TEMPLE EMANU-EL, 1364 49th Street, 1908. Fig. 63.

Designed for the pioneer Jewish community of Borough Park, this is the best example of Georgian synagogue architecture in Brooklyn. The temple has maintained its high standard of community service throughout the years. David Koussevitski is the cantor of the congregation.

FIRST CONGREGATION ANSHE SFARD, 4502 Fourteenth Avenue, 1915. Figs. 64 and 65; Inside Back Cover, Bottom.

The doors of this synagogue are open for prayer and study from 5 A.M. to 10 P.M. every day of the year—a true service to the Jewish community! The ark, executed in crafted wood and plaster, is a fine work of art. On its sides are portrayed the musical instruments used in Biblical times (*fig. 65*). The doors of the ark are inscribed with an abbreviation of the High Holy Day prayer *Avinu Malkaynu*.

CONGREGATION SHOMREI EMUNAH, 5202 Fourteenth Avenue, 1910. Fig. 66.

Traces of Louis Sullivan's approach to the Romanesque Revival style are evident in the facade of this synagogue. The interior, however, was refurbished with Art Deco furnishings. True eclecticism.

BOROUGH PARK *SHTEEBLECH*. Fig. 67.

The majority of Borough Park's 200 synagogues are small storefront or renovated residential *shteeblech* (small rooms, in Yiddish). On the corner of Fifteenth Avenue and 43rd Street alone there are no less than four of them! As a result, it is now Borough Park that is called the "Jerusalem of America."

CONGREGATION BETH TORAH, 1061 Ocean Parkway, 1969; Richard Foster, architect. Figs. 68 and 69.

A part of the Syrian community of Flatbush, the congregation has roots stemming from the days when it fled the Spanish Inquisition, first to Italy, then to Turkey, and finally to Syria. The majority of this Sephardic community immigrated to the United States at the turn of the century. Although Foster (who also designed the New York State Pavilion at the World's Fair of 1964) uses a modern style here, the ancient Sephardic arrangement prevails: reading table in the center, seating parallel to the table and the ark against the eastern wall.

EAST MIDWOOD JEWISH CENTER, 1625 Ocean Avenue, 1929. Fig. 70.

CONGREGATION B'NAI ISRAEL, 3007 Ocean Avenue, 1930. Figs. 71 and 72.

The interior of the synagogue, built during the Depression, reflects traditional East European folk arts and crafts, the ark and *bimah* in particular. The mural depicts scenes of the Holy Land.

SEA BREEZE JEWISH CENTER (CONGREGATION GEMILAS CHESED), 311 Sea Breeze Avenue, 1901. Fig. 73.

In the nineteenth century, during the hot summer months, city residents flocked to Brooklyn's seashore areas—to Brighton, Bath and Coney Island Beaches. After the season, the summer synagogues would close as the Jewish community returned to New York. At the turn of the century, however, people realized that the beauties of the area could be enjoyed year-round and developed the communities, along with their synagogues, into permanent establishments.

CONGREGATION SHAARE ZEDEK, 2301 Mermaid Avenue, 1920. Fig. 74.

CONGREGATION KNESES ISRAEL, 3803 Nautilus Avenue, 1924. Figs. 75 and 76.

On the westernmost tip of Coney Island is the private community of Sea Gate. A resident's pass is required for entry. At the turn of the century the area was a millionaires' preserve with restrictions placed against Jewish residency. Today it is 75 percent Jewish, a 12-foot-high fence protecting the residents from outsiders. Congregation Kneses Israel is the largest synagogue in the section.

Beth Elohim, 274 Keap Street. 39. Cornerstone with date according to Hebrew reckoning.

40

Beth Elohim. 40. Facade of the original building constructed in 1876.
Ohav Sholom, 135 Thatford Avenue. 41. Exterior of the 1906 Shtetl Revival structure (demolished), once the largest in Brownsville.

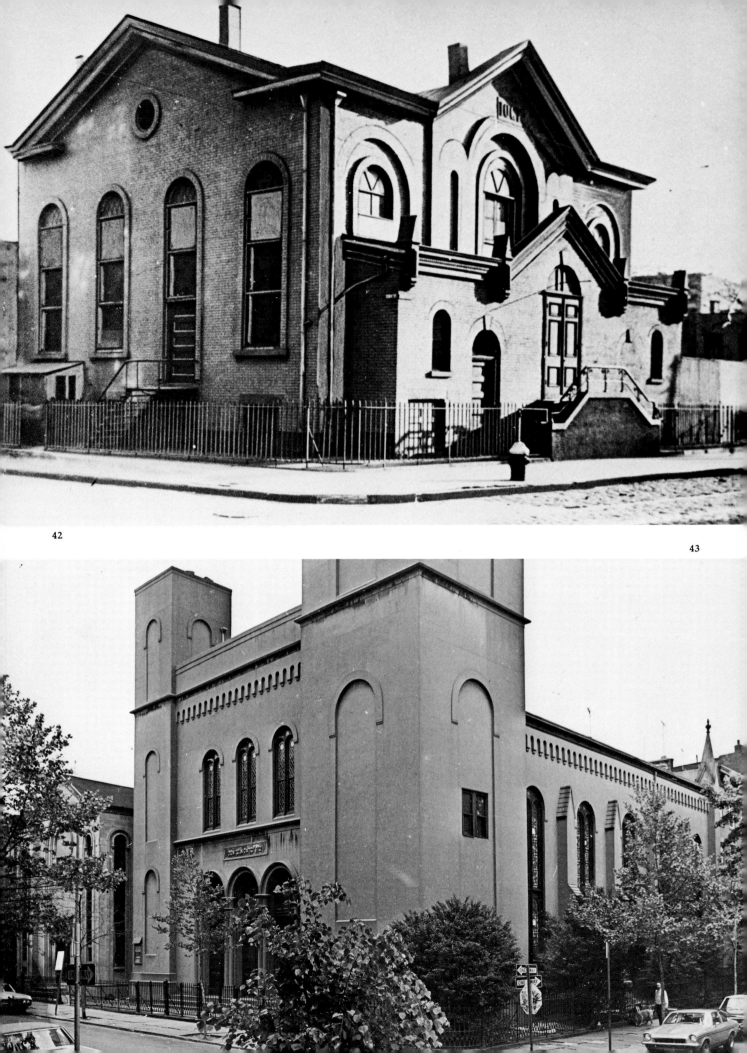

42

43

44

בית ישראל אנשי אמת

Baith Israel Anshei Emes, 236 Kane Street. 42. First structure, at the southeast corner of State Street and Boerum Place (demolished). 43. Exterior of the building purchased in 1905 on Kane Street, formerly the Trinity Lutheran Church. 44. Detail of the facade. 45. View of the interior.

46

48

49

Agudas Achim B'nai Jacob, 503 Glenmore Avenue. 46. Exterior of the building constructed in 1921.

Chevre Chayei Adam, 336 Ashford Street. 47. The turn-of-the-century building, originally constructed as a church, serves as a church once again.

Sinai, 24 Arlington Avenue. 48. The synagogue is the last one still functioning in Brownsville.

Ohab Sholom, 19 Varet Street. 49. View of the celebration of the opening of the building in 1905.

50

51

52

53

Shaare Zedek, Kingston Avenue and Park Place. 50. Exterior of the Crown Heights synagogue, now a church. **Brooklyn Jewish Center,** 667 Eastern Parkway. 51. Exterior view of the second Jewish Center constructed in the United States (1920). 52. Interior, showing stairway. 53. Cantor Richard Tucker, who became a renowned operatic tenor.

54

55

56

57

Union Temple, 17 Eastern Parkway. 54. An architect's rendering shows the community house with the addition of a temple structure on the left.
Park Slope Jewish Center, Eighth Avenue and 14th Street. 55. Exterior.
Beth Elohim, Eighth Avenue and Garfield Place. 56. Principal facade. 57. Artist's rendering of the interior.

Temple Beth El, 4802 Fifteenth Avenue. 58. First structure, in the Shtetl Revival style, 4022 Twelfth Avenue, 1906. 59. Present structure, 4802 Fifteenth Avenue.

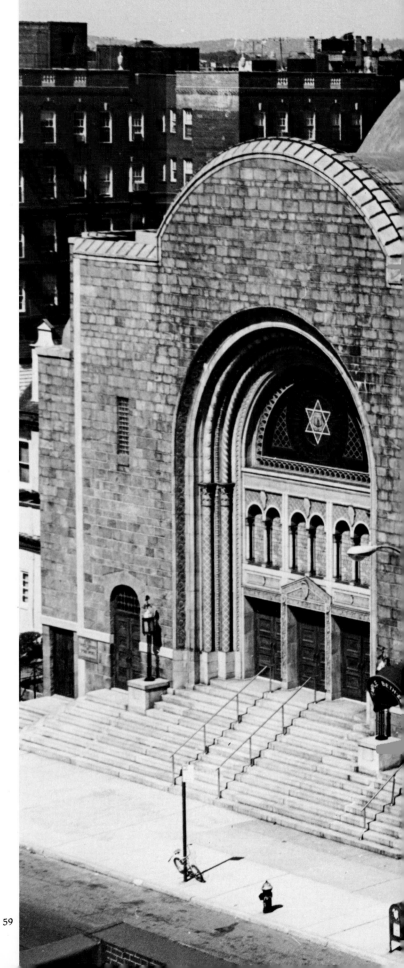

61

Temple Beth El. 60. Interior of the Moorish Revival
auditorium. 61. Detail of the balcony and ceiling.

63

Torath Moshe, Tenth Avenue and 43rd Street.
62. View of the terra-cotta facade.
Emanu-El, 1364 49th Street. 63. The exterior is a fine example of Georgian architecture.

64

Anshe Sfard, 4502 Fourteenth Avenue. 64. View of the structure's exterior. 65. Detail of the wood-and-plaster ark.
Shomrei Emunah, 5202 Fourteenth Avenue. 66. The facade is Romanesque Revival; the interior is Art Deco.
Borough Park shteeblech. 67. Several of Borough Park's many storefront synagogues.

65

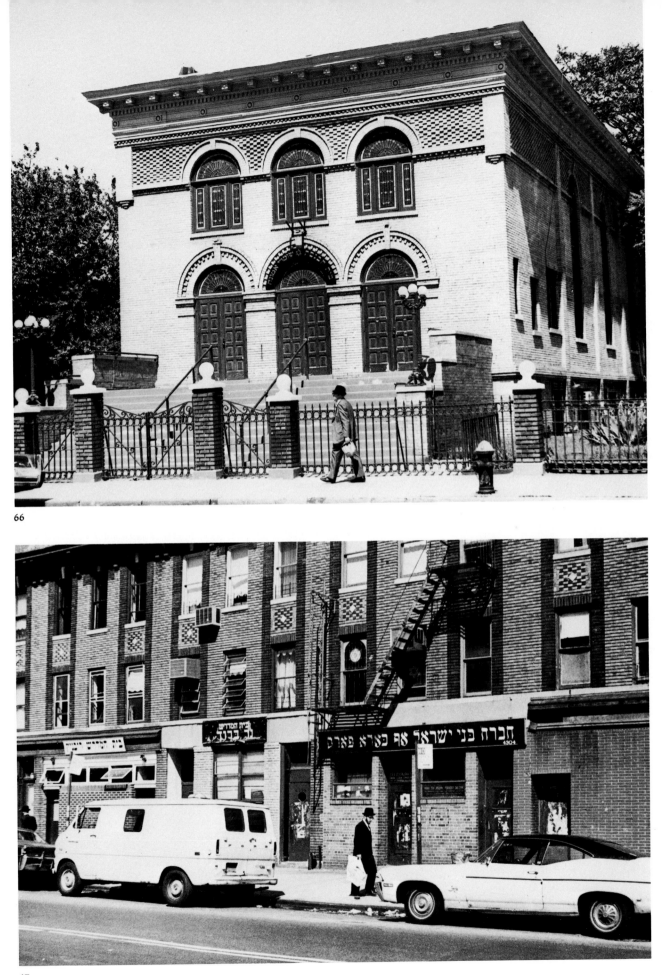

66

67

68

69

Beth Torah, 1061 Ocean Parkway. 68. Although the interior is modern, it retains a Sephardic arrangement. 69. The structure's modernistic facade.

70

71

72

East Midwood Jewish Center, 1625 Ocean Avenue. 70. View of the exterior.
B'nai Israel, 3007 Ocean Avenue. 71. The sanctuary reveals the influence of East European folk art.
72. Exterior.

73

74

75

Sea Breeze Jewish Center, 311 Sea Breeze Avenue. 73. View of the structure's exterior.
Shaare Zedek, 2301 Mermaid Avenue. 74. The synagogue and its neighborhood.
Kneses Israel, 3803 Nautilus Avenue. 75. The synagogue is Sea Gate's largest. 76. Interior view.

76

The Bronx

The Jewish settlement of the Bronx developed in a series of northward migrations. Although there was a small community in the 1840s, it was not until the late 1880s, with the extension of Manhattan's elevated railways, that considerable Jewish settlement was established. The first major Bronx Jewish community was located in the South Bronx in such neighborhoods as Mott Haven, Tremont and Morrisania. The first synagogue in the Bronx, Temple Adath Israel, was organized by German Jews in 1889. The original building on East 169th Street, near Third Avenue, is still extant (fig. 77).

The completion of extensive subway and elevated lines between 1904 and 1940 spurred the transplantation of established Jewish communities of the Lower East Side and Harlem to newly developed sections in the Bronx. Such communities as Fordham, Gun Hill Road and Parkchester became the fashionable areas. For a person to live in an Art Deco apartment building on the Grand Concourse in the 1920s was equivalent to being a member of high society. The Mount Eden Jewish Center, built in 1926, was one of the exclusive congregations in the Bronx (figs. 85–87). In 1930, the Jewish population of the Bronx reached its peak, with a total of 585,000.

After World War II there was a mass migration from the South and Central Bronx because of rapidly deteriorating neighborhoods, the construction of the Cross-Bronx Expressway and the availability of good, inexpensive housing in the suburbs. The abandoned neighborhoods were left to decay and the synagogues were usually sold to black or Hispanic churches. The South Bronx today resembles postwar Berlin, with block after block of burned-out shells of once-elegant apartment buildings.

The remaining Jews of the South and Central Bronx, not wishing to leave the borough, moved to the northernmost communities of Riverdale and Pelham Bay. Co-op City is the last major Jewish settlement in the borough. The huge cooperative housing development consists of 35 apartment towers covering 210 acres in the northeast Bronx. There are six synagogues within the housing complex, serving its 60,000 inhabitants (fig. 88). About 140,000 Jews still live in the borough.

TEMPLE ADATH ISRAEL, Grand Concourse and East 169th Street, 1927, Figs. 77 and 78.
    The first synagogue built by the congregation, organized by German Jews in 1889, is the oldest in the Bronx (fig. 77). The structure at 551 East 169th Street now houses a church. The congregation's second home (fig. 78) has also become a church, the members having left the area as the Grand Concourse deteriorated. The congregation merged with the Conservative Synagogue of Riverdale in the 1960s.

BETH HAMEDRASH HAGADOL ADATH ISRAEL OF THE BRONX, Forest Avenue and East 158th Street, 1913. Fig. 80. 1590 Washington Avenue, 1926. Fig. 79.
    Changing neighborhoods forced the congregation to shift locations. When the Cross-Bronx Expressway disrupted the area, many of the congregation's members moved to the northern sections of the Bronx or to the suburbs.

MONTEFIORE CONGREGATION, 764 Hewitt Place, 1906. Fig. 81.
    Now a church, the building stands as a monument to the Jewish residents who once thrived in the South Bronx.

CONGREGATION SONS OF ISRAEL, 777 East 178th Street, 1917. Figs. 82 and 83.
    The central and south Bronx now resemble Berlin at the end of World War II—block after block is in a state of rubble and ruin. The remains of once-elegant apartment houses and formerly glorious synagogues are found in this totally neglected part of the city. The synagogue was firebombed in 1975 and has since been demolished.

SINAI CONGREGATION, 951 Stebbins Avenue, 1911. Fig. 84.
    The Neoclassical facade remains relatively unchanged; reliefs of the menorah and Stars of David are still visible. But the congregation has moved from the area and the building has been sold to a church.

MOUNT EDEN CENTER, 16 West Mount Eden Avenue, 1926. Figs. 85–87.
    The Grand Concourse was designed in 1892 by Louis Risse. Named the Speedway Concourse, it led to the borough's parks from Manhattan. In later years its many luxury Art Deco apartment buildings housed well-to-do Jewish residents who promenaded up and down the boulevard in their best attire on the Sabbath. The Mount Eden Center was one of the grand synagogues of the area—the place to hold an affair or wedding. The neighborhood had changed changed dramatically by the time the building was sold in 1982.

CO-OP CITY, 1968–70. Fig. 88.
    The world's largest co-op housing development, Co-op City has a total population of 75,000 and as many Jews as Atlanta, New Orleans, Des Moines and Wilmington put together. A community unto itself, it contains six separate synagogues. Many of the residents are elderly, many middle-class. A large number moved to Co-op City from the older, decaying areas of the Bronx.

SALANTER AKIBA RIVERDALE ACADEMY, 655 West 254th Street, 1974; Caudill, Rowlett, Scott, Assocs., architect. Figs. 89–91.
    Three Hebrew day schools have been literally merged under one roof, for there are no walls between the classrooms of this elementary school. The sloped roof (fig. 90) provides every class space with a view across the Hudson River. The chapel (fig. 89) is designed as a theater in the round. Before entering the chapel, students pass a memorial to the Holocaust (fig. 91). The academy occupies the land of an estate where conductor Arturo Toscanini lived.

77

78

79

Adath Israel. 77. First structure, the oldest synagogue in the Bronx. **78.** Exterior of the congregation's second home, Grand Concourse and East 169th Street.
Beth Hamedrash Hagadol Adath Israel. 79. The congregation moved to this, its second structure, at 1590 Washington Avenue, when its original neighborhood changed.

80

Beth Hamedrash Hagadol Adath Israel. 80. First structure, Forest Avenue and East 158th Street.
Montefiore Congregation, 764 Hewitt Place. 81. View
of the facade.

82

83

Sons of Israel, 777 East 178th Street. 82. Exterior of the synagogue (demolished). 83. The interior in ruins.
Sinai Congregation, 951 Stebbins Avenue. 84. The Neoclassical facade bears plaques with Jewish motifs in relief.

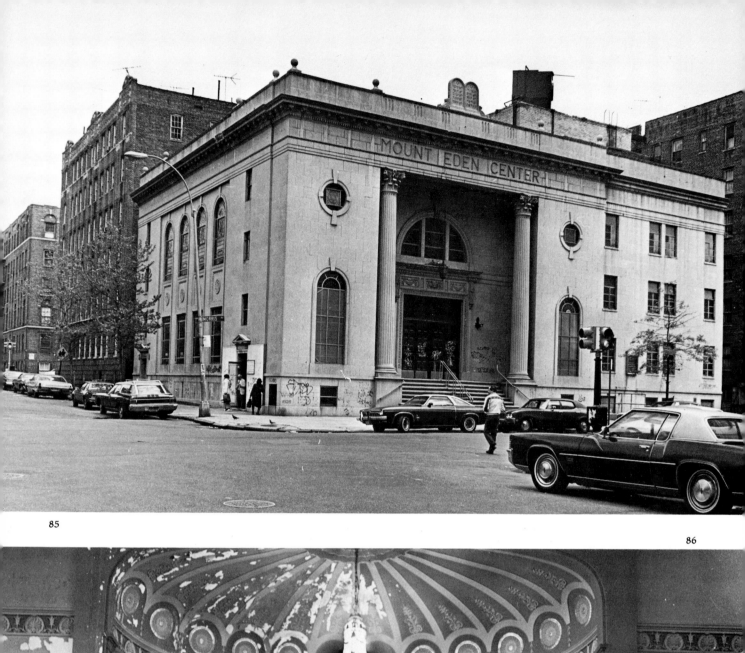

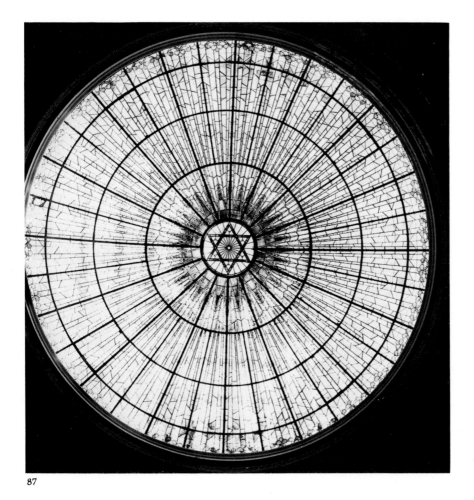

87

Mount Eden Center, 16 West Mount Eden Avenue. 85. Exterior of the synagogue, for many years one of the most prestigious in the Bronx. 86. The sanctuary. 87. A stained-glass window.
Co-op City. 88. The largest co-op housing development in the world contains six synagogues.

89

Salanter Akiba Riverdale Academy, 655 West 254th Street. 89. Exterior of the circular chapel. 90. The sloping roof of the classroom area. 91. The Holocaust memorial. Names of concentration camps are inscribed on the central panel.

90

91

Queens

Although Jews have lived in Queens since 1759, it was not until after the Civil War that a Jewish community developed. Jewish peddlers, storekeepers and a few farmers settled in such areas as Jamaica, Flushing and Newtown (later called Jackson Heights). One section of Forest Hills stands on what was known in the early 1870s as Goldberg's dairy farm.

German-Jewish vacationers organized the first synagogue in the Rockaways at the turn of the century. The first structure, Temple of Israel, was built in 1900 in the Hammels. The original Shtetl Revival structure, destroyed by fire in 1920, was replaced by the present three-story brick edifice. Before Temple Israel, a Reform congregation, was organized in 1908, services were held over the dry-goods store of A. Louis Nebenzahl, a Far Rockaway merchant who peddled dry goods throughout Long Island in the 1880s. Temple Israel built its first structure in Far Rockaway in 1911 but moved across the city line to Lawrence (Nassau County) in 1930 to become a leading Reform congregation on Long Island.

The early summer-resort Jewish settlements in the Rockaways—Arverne, Rockaway Beach, Belle Harbor and Neponsit—have since become year-round communities. The oldest surviving synagogue structure in the Rockaways (and in Queens), Congregation Derech Emunah, was built in 1904. The luxury resort hotels that once surrounded it have been demolished. This building has recently been designated an official New York City landmark.

Other early Jewish settlements in Queens include such communities as Astoria (1894), Corona (1900) and Long Island City (1904). The completion of the Queensboro Bridge in 1909 and the subsequent construction of the elevated railroad lines sparked new Jewish settlement in Woodside, Queens Village, Hollis and Sunnyside.

The opening of the New York World's Fair in 1939 and the extension of the Independent subway line brought thousands of visitors to Queens. They liked what they saw and decided to settle in the borough. The 1940s and 1950s witnessed a mass migration from deteriorating neighborhoods in Manhattan, Brooklyn and the Bronx and the creation of instant Jewish neighborhoods in Forest Hills, Rego Park, Kew Gardens and Elmhurst.

The Jewish population of Queens is estimated at 225,000, including about 75,000 recent Israeli immigrants, so it has been called the "fourth city of Israel." There are about 135 synagogues in the borough.

TEMPLE OF ISRAEL, 188 Beach 84th Street, 1900. Figs. 92 and 93.
The oldest congregation in Queens, Temple of Israel built its first synagogue (*fig. 92*) in 1900 in Shtetl Revival style to serve the Rockaway summer resort of the Hammels. The structure was destroyed by fire in 1920, but the congregation built its present three-story brick structure on the same site in 1921.

CONGREGATION DERECH EMUNAH, 199 Beach 67th Street, 1904; William A. Lambert, architect. Figs. 94–96.
This synagogue is an impressive reminder of the importance of this section of the Rockaways during the early twentieth century, when the area was a stylish Jewish summer-resort colony known as Arverne-by-the-Sea. Designed in the elegant Neo-Georgian style, the shingle-sided synagogue was erected to meet the needs of the rapidly growing Jewish community nearby. The building has been declared an official New York City Historic Landmark.

TEMPLE ISRAEL, Central Avenue and Winchester Place (Lawrence, New York), 1930; S. Brian Baylinson, architect. Fig. 97.
The German-Jewish vacationers who began spending summers in the seaside villages on the Rockaway Peninsula in the 1880s organized what were probably the first services in Queens. Held over the dry-goods store of A. Louis Nebenzahl, who had peddled all over Long Island in the 1880s, they grew into Temple Israel, which was organized in 1908 in Far Rockaway. In 1930, the congregation moved four blocks across the city line to build its elegant brick temple in Lawrence, New York.

TEMPLE BETH EL OF ROCKAWAY BEACH, Rockaway Boulevard and Beach 121st Street, 1925; Maurice Courland, architect. Figs. 98 and 99.

CONGREGATION KNESSETH ISRAEL (THE WHITE SHUL), 728 Empire Avenue, 1964; Kelly & Gruzen, architects. Fig. 100.

This synagogue was designed as a theater in the round to emphasize the theme of the Torah as the center of Jewish life.

FIRST INDEPENDENT HEBREW CONGREGATION (AHAVAS ISRAEL), 90–21 160th Street, 1905. Figs. 101 and 102.

Although Jews had lived in what is now Queens before the American Revolution, and were doing business in Jamaica, Flushing and Newtown (Jackson Heights), there were no synagogues built until the early 1900s. Congregation Ahavas Israel built its Shtetl Revival synagogue near the Long Island Railroad terminal in Jamaica. The neighborhood has changed dramatically, and the younger Jewish residents have long since moved away. The building has been sold to a church, but the delicately handcrafted ark will be dismantled, restored and reassembled in another synagogue.

FREE SYNAGOGUE OF FLUSHING, 41–60 Kissena Boulevard, 1926; Maurice Courland, architect. Fig. 103.

The congregation was organized in 1917. Its first structure, later used as its community house, had been designed by Stanford White and was purchased in 1921. Bernard Contor, the congregation's first rabbi, was called to the pulpit in 1920. Later that year, while overseas with a unit of the Joint Distribution committee, he was murdered by bandits in the Ukraine.

TEMPLE GATES OF PRAYER, 143-51 Roosevelt Avenue, 1921. Fig. 104.

The first Jewish organization in Flushing, where there had been local Jewish merchants since the 1880s, was Temple Gates of Prayer. In 1921, after the construction of subway lines in Queens opened up the borough, the congregation built this two-story brick synagogue, which still stands. The main sanctuary of the congregation is housed in a contemporary structure around the corner.

FOREST HILLS JEWISH CENTER, 106–06 Queens Boulevard. Fig. 105.

Many Jews from Manhattan, the Bronx and Brooklyn first visited Queens during the 1939 World's Fair and found it attractive. New rapid transit lines and new highways made it easy to reach Queens from the older sections of the other boroughs. After World War II, when returning veterans found a housing shortage in their home neighborhoods, they poured into the new apartment houses that were rising in Queens.

INTERNATIONAL SYNAGOGUE, John F. Kennedy International Airport, 1963; Bloch & Hesse, architects. Figs. 106 and 107.

Designed as a sculptural abstraction, this synagogue blends in well with its environment, where architectural masterpieces have been assembled as a showcase for the international traveler. Some of the architects represented by work at Kennedy Airport include I. M. Pei, Eero Saarinen, and Skidmore, Owings & Merrill. The interior rendition of the Ten Commandments on bronze plaques *(fig. 107)* was designed by world-renowned artist Chaim Gross. The spatial design of the interior closely resembles that of North America's first synagogue, the Mill Street Synagogue. Run under the auspices of the New York Board of Rabbis, the synagogue is intended to serve the needs of over 3000 Jewish workers at the airport. It is closed on the Sabbath and on all Jewish holidays!

Temple of Israel, 188 Beach 84th Street. 92. First structure, destroyed by fire in 1920. 93. Facade of the present structure. **Derech Emunah**, 199 Beach 67th Street. 94. The building, in a Neo-Georgian style, is a New York City Historic Landmark.

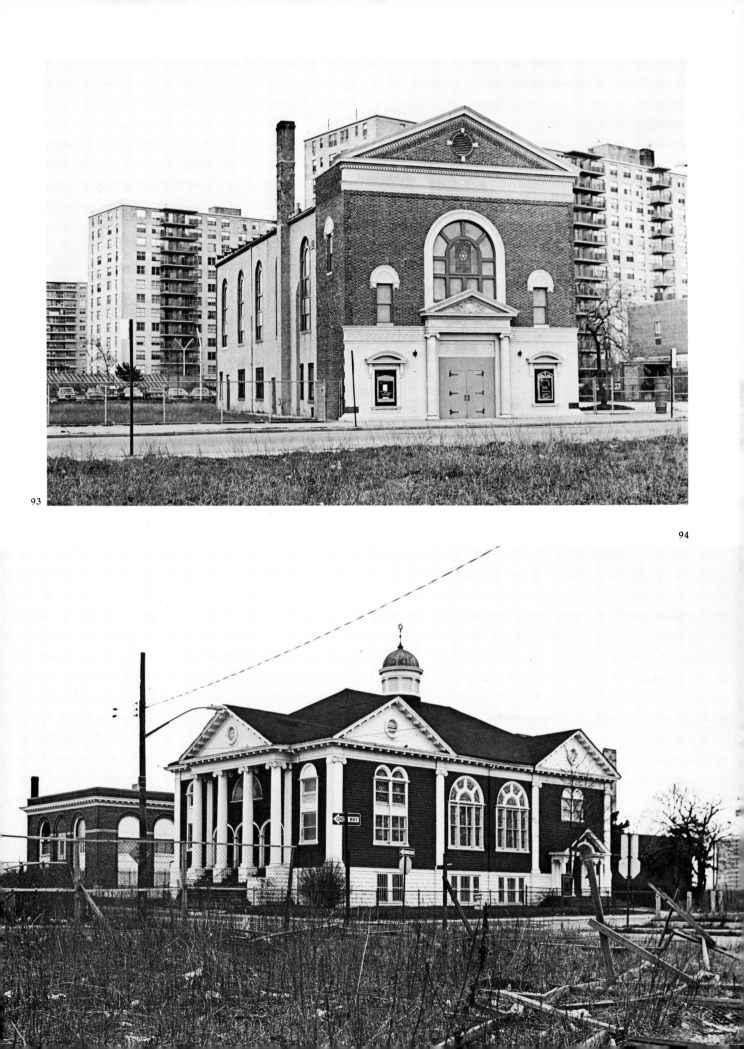

95

96

97

Derech Emunah. 95. Detail of the facade. 96. The sanctuary.
Temple Israel, Central Avenue and Winchester Place, Lawrence. 97. Exterior of the elegant brick temple. The congregation moved from Far Rockaway in 1930.

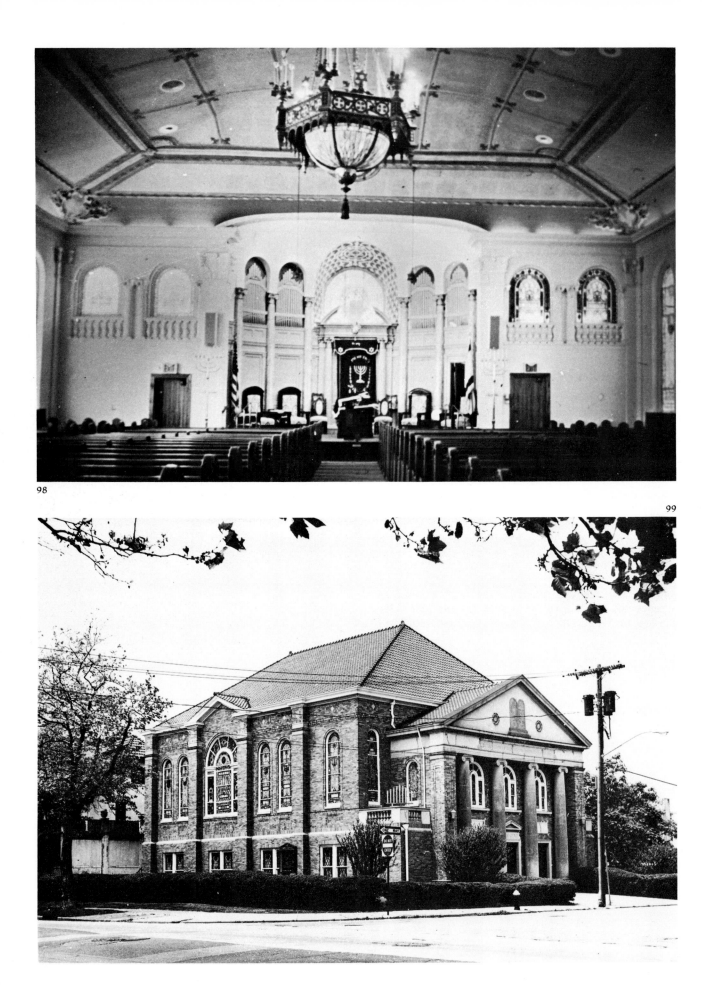

100

Beth El, Rockaway Boulevard and Beach 121st Street.
98. Interior. 99. View of the exterior.
Knesseth Israel, 728 Empire Avenue. 100. The interior
reflects a "theater in the round" concept.

101

First Independent Hebrew Congregation, 90–21 160th Street. 101. The Shtetl Revival facade, constructed in 1905. 102. The handcrafted ark dominates the sanctuary.

Free Synagogue of Flushing, 41–60 Kissena Boulevard. 103. An aerial view of the exterior reveals the size of the dome.

104

105

107

Temple Gates of Prayer, 143–51 Roosevelt Avenue. 104. Exterior of the 1921 structure.
Forest Hills Jewish Center, 106–06 Queens Boulevard. 105. The synagogue's menorah.
International Synagogue, John F. Kennedy Airport. 106. Exterior, designed as a sculptural abstraction. 107. The Ten Commandments were rendered in bronze by artist Chaim Gross.

Staten Island

Staten Island (the borough of Richmond) has had a Jewish community since the 1850s. The first settlements were in St. George, Port Richmond, Tompkinsville, New Brighton (all located near the Staten Island ferry landing) and Tottenville (in the southern end of the island).

The first congregation, B'nai Jeshurun, was organized in 1887. Its three-story frame synagogue was built in 1891 in Tompkinsville. As the community expanded, a second congregation, Agudath Achim Anshe Chesed, was organized in 1900 and built its synagogue in New Brighton in 1907. Another congregation, Temple Emanu-El, built its synagogue in 1907 in the Port Richmond section, styling it in the Neoclassical mode of Jeffersonian architecture.

In 1916, when there were about 3500 Jews in Staten Island, a fourth congregation, Temple Tifereth Israel (Hebrew Alliance), was organized in Stapleton. Its three-story brick synagogue was built in 1927. Congregation Ahavath Israel was organized in 1918 in Tottenville; its two-story frame synagogue was built in 1932.

Prior to 1964, the Staten Island ferry provided the only direct link to the rest of New York City. The opening of the Verrazano-Narrows Bridge from Brooklyn to Staten Island in 1964 brought a building boom and an influx of Jewish residents. New Jewish communities developed in Willowbrook, Eltingville and Great Kills. The anticipated mass exodus from the other boroughs to Staten Island, however, failed to materialize. Geography and limited transportation facilities have still kept Staten Island's population and its Jewish communities small. The Jewish population of Staten Island is about 21,000 and there are about 20 synagogues.

NEW BRIGHTON JEWISH CONGREGATION (ORIGINALLY CONGREGATION B'NAI JESHURUN), 199 Victory Boulevard, 1891. Figs. 108 and 109.

The first Jew to settle on Staten Island was Moses Greenwald, an immigrant from Germany. The first Jewish child known to have been born on the island was his son Abram (1857). But it was not until the last two decades of the nineteenth century that a larger community began to emerge, concentrated on the east shore, near the landing of the ferry to New York City. In 1887, at Tompkinsville, a group incorporated the first congregation on Staten Island, B'nai Jeshurun, and built its three-story frame synagogue in 1891 (fig. 108). The congregation remained in the building until 1971, when it sold it to a local nursery school and moved to its present site in Westerleigh. The new building (fig. 109) was constructed in 1974. In 1978 plans were made to restore the original building as a functioning synagogue and to have it listed as a City Historic Landmark.

TEMPLE EMANU-EL, 984 Post Avenue, 1907; Harry W. Pelcher, architect. Figs. 110 and 111.

The building is a small-town version of a Classical Revival facade: heavy columns and pediment, octagonal domed cupola, even the carefully spelled name in relief over the entrance—complete with hyphen. Yet there is a strength of purpose in both the innocent pretentiousness of the portions of the street facade painted white and the more straightforward cladding of the remainder of the edifice's wood frame—shingles stained a deep forest green. Temple Emanu-El is a wonderful relic of this community's earlier days.

CONGREGATION AGUDATH ACHIM ANSHE CHESED, 641 Delafield Avenue. Figs. 112 and 113.

In 1900, the expanding community, feeling the need for a second congregation, incorporated Agudath Achim at New Brighton, at 386 Jersey Street (fig. 112). But in 1970 the changing neighborhood forced the congregation to move and the Faith Methodist Church in West Brighton (fig. 113) was purchased and renovated to meet the religious requirements of the congregation.

CONGREGATION TIFERETH ISRAEL, Wright Street near Duzer Street, 1927. Fig. 114.

As the community grew, additional congregations were founded. Tifereth Israel was organized in 1916 at Stapleton as the Hebrew Alliance, renaming itself in 1927, when the synagogue was erected. The neighborhood having deteriorated, in 1977 the congregation sold the building to a church and merged with Congregation B'nai Jeshurun.

CONGREGATION AHAVATH ISRAEL, 7630 Amboy Road, 1932. Fig. 115.

The congregation was organized in Tottenville, the southernmost town of Staten Island, in 1918. Services were held in the homes of members until the frame synagogue was built. The region around Tottenville remains relatively unspoiled, with thick forests and an occasional farmhouse.

TEMPLE ISRAEL REFORM CONGREGATION, 315 Forest Avenue, 1964; Percival Goodman, architect. Fig. 116.

Organized in 1948, Temple Israel's initial services were held in the Sailor's Snug Harbor. After their second home, the Gans mansion, was destroyed by fire, the present building was erected. It has a flexible floor plan on the sanctuary level and classroom and meeting facilities on its lower level.

ARDEN HEIGHTS BOULEVARD JEWISH CENTER, 1766 Arthur Kill Road. Fig. 117.

The opening of the Verrazano-Narrows Bridge in 1964, linking Brooklyn and Staten Island, created a building boom on the island and a considerable influx of Jewish residents to such new neighborhoods as Arden Heights, Willowbrook and New Springville.

YOUNG ISRAEL OF STATEN ISLAND, 835 Forest Hill Road, 1970. Fig. 118.

B'nai Jeshurun of Staten Island, 199 Victory Boulevard. 108. The original structure of Staten Island's first congregation at Tompkinsville, now owned by the New Brighton Jewish Congregation. 109. View of the new building constructed in 1974.

Emanu-El, 984 Post Avenue. 110. Exterior. 111. Interior of the temple's sanctuary.

110

111

112

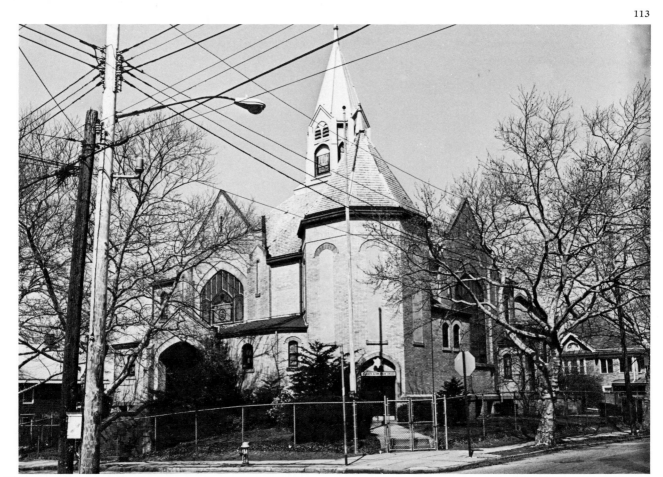

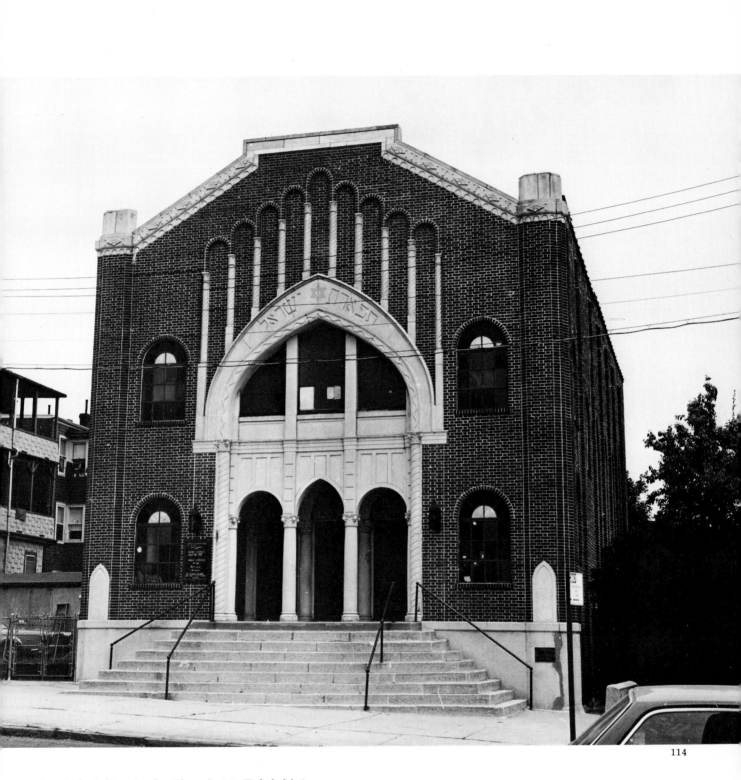

114

Agudath Achim Anshe Chesed, 641 Delafield Avenue.
112. First structure, 386 Jersey Street. 113. The present
structure, a former church.
Tifereth Israel, Wright Street near Duzer Street. 114.
Facade of the building, now a church.

115

116

117

118

Ahavath Israel, 7630 Amboy Road. 115. The synagogue stands in a wooded location.
Temple Israel, 315 Forest Avenue. 116. The structure has a flexible floor plan.
Arden Heights Boulevard Jewish Center, 1766 Arthur Kill Road. 117. View of the exterior and grounds.
Young Israel of Staten Island, 835 Forest Hill Road. 118. The modern structure's exterior.

BIBLIOGRAPHY

Jewish Landmarks of New York, Postal and Koppman, Fleet Press, 1978.
A.I.A. Guide to New York City, White and Willensky, Collier Books, 1978.
The Universal Jewish Encyclopedia, 1948.
Brownsville, A. F. Landesman, Block Publishers, 1969.
Brooklyn Daily Eagle Almanac, 1889–1929.
Recent American Synagogue Architecture – Catalogue, The Jewish Museum of New York, 1963.
The Synagogue, Brian de Breffny, Macmillan Publishing Co., 1978.
History of Brooklyn Jewry, Samuel P. Abelow, Scheba Publishing, 1937.
Two Hundred Years of American Synagogue Architecture – Catalogue, American Jewish Historical Society, 1976.
When Harlem was Jewish, 1870–1930, J. Gurock, Columbia University Press, 1979.
Encyclopedia Judaica, Keter Publishing House, Jerusalem Ltd., 1972.
Maimonides – Mishnah Torah, Laws of Prayer (Chapter II).

PHOTOGRAPHIC CREDITS

Brooklyn Public Library: 12, 40, 42, 45, 49, 52, 54, 57, 58, 92.
Museum of the City of New York: 19 (Byron), 29, 31.
Congregation Ohab Zedek Archives: 30.
Temple Emanu-El Archives: 10, 17, 18.
Congregation B'nai Jeshurun Archives: 8.
Congregation Shearith Israel Archives: 2.